Glasshouses

Stuart Barnes was born in Hobart, Tasmania, and educated at Monash University. He was runner-up for the 2014 Arts Queensland Thomas Shapcott Poetry Prize. Since 2013 he has lived in Central Queensland and been poetry editor for *Tincture Journal*. *Glasshouses* is his first book.

Praise for *Glasshouses*

'A beautiful and sophisticated collection of poems. Drawing on a number of complex techniques … the manuscript presents a deeply poetic sensibility at work.'

—Judges' comments, Thomas Shapcott Poetry Prize

'Man moves in a world made of things, beings and events.
And things, beings and events move in the mind of man.
Living in this half-transparent state triggers poetic reactions,
strong and beautiful poems like the ones you'll find in
Stuart Barnes' *Glasshouses*.'

—Sjón

THE ARTS QUEENSLAND THOMAS SHAPCOTT POETRY PRIZE SERIES

Lidija Cvetkovic *War Is Not the Season for Figs*
Jaya Savige *latecomers*
Nathan Shepherdson *Sweeping the Light Back into the Mirror*
Angela Gardner *Parts of Speech*
Sarah Holland-Batt *Aria*
Felicity Plunkett *Vanishing Point*
Rosanna Licari *An Absence of Saints*
Vlanes *Another Babylon*
Nicholas Powell *Water Mirrors*
Rachael Briggs *Free Logic*
David Stavanger *The Special*
Krissy Kneen *Eating My Grandmother: a grief cycle*

WINNER
OF THE
2015
THOMAS
SHAPCOTT
POETRY
PRIZE

Stuart Barnes

Glasshouses

UQP

First published 2016 by University of Queensland Press
PO Box 6042, St Lucia, Queensland 4067 Australia

www.uqp.com.au
uqp@uqp.uq.edu.au

Design by Sandy Cull, gogoGingko
Author photograph by Leigh Backhouse
Typeset in 11.5/14 pt Adobe Garamond Pro by Post Pre-press Group, Brisbane
Printed in Australia by McPherson's Printing Group

Queensland Government
Arts Queensland

This project is supported by the Queensland Government through Arts Queensland.

National Library in Australia
Cataloguing-in-Publication data is available at
http://catalogue.nla.gov.au

ISBN 978 0 7022 5413 0 (pbk)
ISBN 978 0 7022 5772 8 (ePDF)
ISBN 978 0 7022 5773 5 (ePub)
ISBN 978 0 7022 5774 2 (Kindle)

University of Queensland Press uses papers that are natural, renewable and recyclable products made from wood grown in sustainable forests. The logging and manufacturing processes conform to the environmental regulations of the country of origin.

Merrily, merrily shall I live now
Under the blossom that hangs on the bough.
—William Shakespeare, *The Tempest*

Bay of Fires'
cockatoos embroider
a crèche of stars

night's deer-sprint to the outdoor
churn's venerable, ineluctable,
dizzying as Virgil

the moon is salubrious,
her vision's sharper than the spectacled flying fox's, her sight
might inscribe similar discs of stillness

Contents

Reflections

Fingal Valley

Nan's budgerigar,
cat fed   squeezing like morning
fog between oxidised barbed
wire and gorse
with an older cousin
and a slug gun

booting sheep skulls
stripped by gusts, our fathers'
1950s snares   swooped by plovers,
daring: 'yellow spurs! forearms
up!'   shooting star-
lings for laughs

another exhausted afternoon:
a hotted-up Torana: another burnout
to Warrant, to Poison
footy, swimming, cricket
on Pop's prized green, putting
with the wrong kind of club

transfixed by sixpence-
riddled heads hooked over the wash-
board   another hand of Patience
and Snap!   the glass swan
brimming with owl-red water
numb on mother-of-pearl veneer

lake   one more theft—
a short-finned eel, writhing
and crackling—from the Esk
squeal of cast-iron frying
pans   slaps on the back   each mouth-
ful of muddy flesh foreign to a south-

erner   on each empty double bed
a leering toilet roll
doll   full moon, mid-
night's deer-sprint to the outdoor
loo   the top bunk's hexagonal wiring sprung,
mattress oozing through cells like honey

The Moon and the Mason Jars

for Ruth Whebell

Purified in stainless stockpots
with black Italian cursives and gilt,
stuffed with smashed green cabbage, sea salt,
yoghurt's

whey; three-quarter revolutions compel
the Latin blanks. From elliptic orbit a well-
versed silver tongue assuages the dish rack's
topsy-turvy characters.

Ebon Cans

In the twinkling of an eye,
in a moment, all is changed
— Gwen Harwood, 'Bone Scan'

In the twinkling of her eye, all is changed:
the small blond child afraid of almost every
thing — father, mother, himself especially —
but books, and paper and pen, awakens

in the vestry where, in four years, the lick
of the oily priest's hand against his thigh
will roil minds. *In the twinkling of an eye*
he'll coil at high school. 'Here's another — quick!

— stuff it in your pocket — it's so important.'
Blackout, blackout — here it comes — his father's
negativity. 'There's zero future

for you as mathematician, doctor.'
Such depths they charge; such queer laughter.
He glances over his shoulder. She mouths *Write*

13

Tzameti, lines to a rondeau, chapters in *The Art of War.* Cards per suit, steps to the gallows, loaves in a baker's dozen. Diners at the Last Supper, gods at Valhalla's banquet, dismemberments of Osiris.
Studio LPs by The Cure, lunar months every calendar year, primary members of The Thirteen Club. Olives, olive leaves, arrows and stars on the Great Seal of the United States. Players in a rugby league team; teenagers starring in *13*, the Broadway musical; letters in Bixby, Oklahoma, the city where Scott Westerfeld's *Midnighters* trilogy, gripped by this troublous number, is set. Syllables till the broken motif of this poem. Lucky for some.

из России

for Therese Stuart

Alitalia: hazy, like Nan & Pop's … Rome: the taxis! the
cats! … Moscow's gilt mocks, McDonald's', too: one
goddamn Big Mac "meal" = one month's wage! … Fifty
dead presidents for genuine black-market sailor shirt: itch
-y, made from wool … Gypsies nearly whoosh our bus
in Pushkin … Saint Petersburg → Karelia train star-red,
ash-blond scouts snooze like speechless speech marks …
Lake Ladoga: icebox; MOSQUITOES; white nights be-
wilder Siberian cedars … Kath & I boomerang to de-
mountables: 'Il y a un beau garçon là-bas': Ilya's cheeks
borscht-pink … T's headphones: The Cure's 'Fire in
Cairo' … **I ♥ zh** … ~~Homesick for Hobart …~~ с любовью

ValproateFluoxetineClonazepam

Every day four purple pills,
four laughing Smarties (cochineals
steamed, boiled, burned alive)
for disguise

a capsule, half ivory,
half peppermint (an elephant's
head severed, a plant's leaves,
flowers crushed) for grunt

another pill, pure
white, quarter-scored,
like the Eucharist,
like a sport

These are the cures that isolate
These are the cures that chill
These are the cures that splice the will
These are the cures that kill

Black Cockatoos

after David Brooks

Red-
tailed Bedouins
of Poetry, black
cockatoos embroider
the sun into us,
seam-rip it asunder.

*

On the Fitzroy's
bank at midday,
cracking seeds of eucalypts
that outrank Council, a hundred
Banksian black cockatoos,
a paroxysm of commas.

*

With their subtler
complex-
ions, the females infinitely
more beautiful
than the ludic-
rously coloured gatherers.

*

The gospel according to the locals:
'Four black cockatoos
kreeing seawards
means four days of rain'
(burkesbackyard.com.au confirms it).
I am not a God-fearing man.

*

Should black cockatoos
know
that theirs are the colours of life?
Indefatigable black
and needlepointed into this
starry orange and yellow.

*

Imprisoned
black cockatoos
long-lived as man
neglectful beneath the same
white sun, its ROYGBIV illusion
destroyed by the tiniest prism.

Horus and Set

for Zachary Humphrey

From his ebony eyrie
the moon is salubrious,
round as the white lotus' root.
The desert's his adversary.

The moon is salubrious
with his godly left eye.
The desert's his adversary,
spiteful, like a hippopotamus.

With his godly left eye
the moon is neither ossuary,
nor spiteful, like a hippopotamus,
a shape-shifting crocodile.

The moon is not an ossuary.
The desert is a troglodyte,
a shape-shifting crocodile.
The moon's a fresh apothecary,

the desert is a troglodyte.
From his ebony eyrie
the moon's a fresh apothecary,
round as the white lotus' root.

another journey by train

at the ≠≠≠≠≠≠≠'s ♥ awaits my Buddha   each
OSIRIS-moulded foot depresses bitumen: Art

Department's 'I C U' *'wanting to watch me*
watching you' a minimal din from **SENNHEISER**   skylines

often smogged
offer

Xi-He's only star,
overblown cerulean

on an almost-identical hue festooned
commandments: When tone sounds, press the ill-

'IIIII C U, following
your every move . . .'

uminated button to open doors. When a second   warning
Please keep doorways clear   Do not lean against, hold or

force open   Donotjumponoroffamoving seat
s must be vacated for use by passengers with

special needs.*
Penalties apply

↓ Yarra platform: a black bicycle, a black roller
-blade, a black skateboard, a black bottle

swing strangely from DICKENSIAN bricks (hot red circles, hot red
slashes overlap i.e. ∅)   ↑ bound: **strictly prohibited. Heavy**

metlink
Welcome

aboard **No feet on seats No ~~offensive~~ language or behaviour**
No smoking No alcohol consumption No graffiti

FOR YOUR SAFETY
During your journey

your behaviour may
be monitored on CCTV

'I feel U watching me now
III C U … wanting me now'

Dissociation

The waiting
lane: a ten-pin's
set, then rocks and
strikes the waxen pine,
snatches
at a metal frame:
a tiger-lily-orange
five-pin
obfuscates
raised lesions:
three candlepins,
cheeks milked of fat,
roll psychic eyes
to lifeless walls
forget forget forget
black bowling balls
and silver scythes
the doctor's
stiff like Wet on
Wellington's
artificial
marble gods:
and I, this scene
too close to the bone,
a classical bystander also.

ENDONE® Oxycodone hydrochloride 5 mg

Blister-white tablet engraved with 'ENDONE'
on one side, break bar the other.
It does not take the place of your doctor
or pharmacist: opium or morphine:
Accident or Emergency.

Store it below ground, above ground, in
an unlocked cupboard. Store it in the bathroom,
store it near the sink. Leave it on every
window sill, leave it in the car. Swallow
it before meals with a glass of nausea.

Do not show your pupils, abnormal,
do not show your restlessness, do not show your goose
-flesh, do not show your fast heart rate, do not show your new
-born child to a doctor or pharmacist.

Reflections

even sunstruck the ribs rise
from Bennelong Point like Arthur C
Clarke's black slab

I storm the frets, stopping
only to whirl when your aperture's
cocked at my spine

this hair's a sand tornado
'ridiculous,' you needle,
'a blond gothic'   no

licks of laughter (Father,
Son, Ghost shedding Prozac), my
Scorpio sting: 'fuck off, Madame Acronym'

*

the ticket snakes
on knotted
wood shoved between twin beds

once
we had no need
for such arpeggiated space

dulled, you insult
my headphones: 'Other
Voices', 'A Reflection', 'Grinding Halt'

Fender-grey,
a seagull pummels crossbows
on the pane

*

three   four   five
raven finished
casts embark Dry Ice

I'm more cleft
than that acoustic-electric
presented by my daddy

in stunting aisles minors gravedigger-
dance and mew
'lovecatsss'

a crèche of stars
weeps plasma at the mutilated
placard of the Harbour

Deep Sea Love

Here's some activity you may have missed:
pompadour-lure hung three days after I
disentangle.
'It misses me.'
The fourth: A lot has happened on
Facebook since you last logged in. And later:
Do you know [famous so-and-so]? You have more
friends on Facebook than you think.
Emboldened,
the fifth: **You have new friends on Facebook.**
'You can never have enough friends!' OM,
MH and two others have their birthday
today on the sixth.
Her photophore
shimmers shimmers shimmers. I bite, dissolving skins.
Parasite, I atrophy to gonads: deep sea
love for my common black devil, my humpback.

Proverbs

A fish always stinks from the elegy down.
Hell hath no fury like metaphor scorned.
The senryū does not change its spots.
You can't get blood out of a trope.

Love of the couplet's the root of all evil.
Procrastination's the thief of metre.
Nothing is certain but stress and narrative.
The darkest stanza's just before the dawn.

The possessive verb catches the worm.
If wishes were similes, beggars would ride.
There's no such thing as bad lyric.

Two odes are better than one.
An acrostic in time saves nine.
From little poems mini-series grow.

I

hardly recognise the trial—twenty-one cycles over the sun—but I know it wasn't child's play. 'Are you—' 'Yes, Mum.' 'You'll fucking die of AIDS.' I apologised—I can only sympathise with the daily rain of brimstone, fire. In artificial air I lay on my side and scrutinised the waverings of your eye—sea-green, curious, terrified—and the contradictory Whys and the cradle-to-grave compliance. Since Friday I've quantified kilometres—one thousand five hundred and seventy, precisely—on a diagram, in my mind. 'This distance requires—' 'Pfft.' Ripely decided. Stupid fruit. My spine's weak also, yet I'm acquiring the art of ballooning the diaphragm. That terrible final telephone call. 'I'd love to be in a relationship with somebody like'—which terrorises—'you'. Crying. Mystified: 'Are you all right?' Dryly: 'Yes, I'm fine, fine, fine.' 'Well then, bye, bye, bye,' you recited. *Poof!* Fire, water: cardinal, fixed. Our rulers Pluto, Mars; our detriment Venus. How do you survive, bonsai? Why why why won't you actualise *oomph*, do you simply ogle lives through that sea-green, curious, terrified eye.

Glasshouses

Sucking dentures, whistling 'A Boy Named Sue',
my father constructed cold frames, terminuses
—one metre x one metre x one metre, four
facets, and a crown, hinged and flat, threaded
with sparkling wire—of the dark Goliath dwarfing
his father's orchard since seventy-seven. Come winter
they'd clack like men across a draughtsboard over
        the phosphorous earth, dilating, for their seedlings,
        the sun.   Every morning I clack my own
kind of cold frame, a mnemonic black letter
mustering catatonia, a blue translucence
(its anaesthetics too stark for naked eyes). *Green*
worms, my father'd whoop, fingers wiggling, tickling
underarms. Mine, like flourishing bruises, purple and burn.

Port Curtis Road's End

The inability to weep furrows the
pit of my gut like a plough. I, a bull's-eye,
Port Curtis Road's end. *Why won't you return my*
calls. Cows gawk. Wind scallops algae-

green water, grass and fingers. Pop … Pop … *Fish?*
My heart, too, is scalloped. The A1, a crane
pirouettes. The iPhone pumps *Let England Shake.*
I scratch at a plump mosquito bite, inner

right knee. My mind pumps also: *Why won't you re-*
turn my calls, return my calls, ret—
Ducks startle, zip the river as though a dredge
were suctioning their webbing. Heehaw. Heehaw.

Hush. Hush. I marvel at my indifference.
I also gawk, at the cows' simplicity.

*

I turn to a gathering murmuration.
Starlings dip below this bridge then boomerang,
passing over easy meat, to Uluru-
shrewd Mount Archer. Dead white gums. Tonight you'll wail

Your neck's burnt, yet proffer no aloe. Bottle-
green shards, hectares and farmhouses. Shadows
crane from left to right, lengthen: I gabble O's,
sculpture a hedge of tiny white stones: Oxy-

codone: bulging disc: *God, I'd kill for a drink.*
Something larger's taken to the air: a rap-
tor, black against unmoving clouds. A foolscap
saccule swishes: Thoroughbred horsehair: a syn-

chronisation: Grey Goose, Raven Ale, Wild Turkey. I
narrow blinders: tropical boondocks widen.

The Rabbit Catcher

after Sylvia Plath

The little thickets were the only place to get to.
The absence of the sea

Set a white, extravagant quiet.
I awaited the great beauty of the gorse—

Unreeling, perfumed,
Ringing the snares with its unction.

It was intent, like torture.
Its dead black spikes

Made a hole in nothing.
And its flowers tasted like vacancy.

10.15 Saturday Night

10.15 on a Saturday night: my
housemate's asleep, Tiger Coils roil an air
wet as whelps (a bitch yelps), Mulder's chest hair
exposes itself like clockwork. Grindr

trills   Bud what ya into   Familiar thrill.
in general? in bed?   Whatevs HAHA
proving his youth. I thumb Olds' 'Bruise Ghazal'.
write, edit, cook, swim, dance; vers   Goosepimples:

You sound SO fucking GAY   Which is nearly
a rehash of the torment of high school:
orange, swollen fags (not jocks, gorgeous, cool)
bashing brainy fags. It's immense, the fear

of gay men. The rage it creates. The sorrow.
To crash tonight's to burn tomorrow.

sad

The venetians creak: fog's tonnage.
Condensation gasps
          on glassy corners, gloomy Xmas
   dec. The butter's thickened in its crock like
dripping. A constellation of barbed starfish rises
from the mug of tea toward the ceiling
   shooting watery cannonballs intermittently
as Hippolytus de Marsiliis' fingers. The iMac, too,
   is punctuated, each poorly catalogued knuckle
   eroded
                    like an Apostle by my salt. Only
I, oddly overlooked, am hardhearted to this
   seasonal affective disorder.

The smile's

i.m. Phyllis Braslin

Queenie's, my Irish grandmother, hazel-eyed
sailor (London–Sydney, *Orama*, Sweet
Sixteen; birth certificate scattered,
1920s), last of Black Hills' currant

farmers (antique weatherboard also
fire-retold); my bold, hazel-eyed mother's;
untold dentists' (bumble of extractions!
not-quite-five impacted wisdoms, four great white super-

numeraries: sharky architecture);
one glum orthodontist's (three years'
halitosis, miniature racks);

'gorgeous!', 'your best feature!'; a sign that you're
the apple of my eye, that in my mind
I'm sticking a fork into the back of my hand.

eggshells

i.m. Nancy Barnes

we smoothed the blooms enclosing diaphanous
atmospheres, scrambling tangerine globes
in the home that seemed miles & miles
away from my home away from Hobart

cackling about this & that, we pipped
through waist-high pasture, tin pail crooning
between us, one hand small & white
on its handle, the other smaller, browning

we embellished the pail with
shelled sweet peas &
sidesplitting broad beans, nacreous
Christmas beetles

while cousins blew
air cells of future selves
with slug guns, Ataris & moon-
shine, we dyed & Bostiked personas

we transformed faults
'Googies!' shook the kitchen
your buttered soldiers
served alongside molten

cups   fifteen years
we walked
on them around my father's
father, your husband

we crushed them with blue fists
that white & brown
confetti we sprinkled
through his glasshouse

colour wheel

i.m. Mervyn Barnes

the American-
barn-red off-centre
timber
shed

trumpeting
through blood &
bone the glasshouse's
yellow stars

the front yard's statue-
sque rooster
screaming blue
murder till blue

in the face
Bay of Fires'
orange lichen,
zinc-creamed lips

a pine plantation's
green rose-
llas   that Tasmanian
tiger snake's

purple
jaw
slurping at the
truck's driver window

quick wound
the moon
poring
whitely over the almanac

spark

i.m. Greg Barnes

'You'll never forget your first cigarette.'
Benson & Hedges. *When only the best*

will do. Nan's kitchen, extendable
laminex table, your favourite uncle,

Jers, patient as the cow you patted, milked
as a little tacker (that dark horse nipped

your fingers, drawing a bloody simper),
from the small black-and-white tele Richie

Benaud's ('*Whoa! Re*mark*able!*') simmering,
'Hurry up, cobber, spark the toxic thing',

shivering despite the five flannel sheets,
alarmed at four by nausea, the silence

of the vacant lot between Pop's pastel-
green house and a third cousin's, the cat's bell.

i won't let the sun go down on me

after Nik Kershaw and for Anthony Hasell

b's for 'brolga!
my first brolga!
i thought they existed solely in
t-shirt-myth …'

c's for crow, monstrously
glossy, plumped at the meat
works for *Cry of the Curlew*

e's for egret, aka
The Stuart Bird,
for (wood pig-)
eon's omnipotence

h is for hawk that has no regard for the
semi-trailer, ambulance, car,
~~kamikaze,~~
only the snake,
devil-may-care,
low on the highway roily & grey,
Hong Kong Orchid's honeyeater,
blue-faced,
topsy-turvy

i's for ibis,
i saw
another bloody mynah,
'i don't know where the birds'll

go when Marcia punk-er-lunks', it's mighty
tempting to scribble Nik on Kershaw
Gardens' entrance sign

k's for
kred-kred-kred-kred
of red-tailed
black cockatoo

v's for verandahs
of butcher-
birds' hooks

w's for
watch a
sulphur-
crested
cockatoo
mosh to
Daft Punk's
'Phoenix'

y's
for Yeppoon's
white-bellied sea
eagle, sus-
pended gloriously
in the ~~metaphor;~~
~~for~~ y such fuss

Five Centos

Cinquecento

The house received all ornaments to grace it,
The walls were of discolour'd jasper-stone,
One window shut, the other open stood,

The time is come, I must depart
        My last thread, I shall perish on the shore;
Ring out your bells, let mourning shows be spread;

Close the Truncke, embalme the Chest,
You should not trust lieutenants in your room,
      Or hawk of the tower:

Sir Charles into my chamber coming in,
Fillet of a fenny snake,
His chilling cold doth heat require;

Oh, what a lantern, what a lamp of light
Avising the bright beams of these fair eyes
    Where Muses (like bees) make their mansion.

Walking Wounded

A land where war seems impossible
I have carried within me a war, and scars,
a blue sepulchral war and secret
                    men-o'-war
a greed for war like love
a frail society scattered by war repeatedly overrun

*

We play war games on the verandahs
of rare champagne, war songs,
war wounds — or something like that…
   You say you mean peace: I say
      peace, blackmail
And bangs and booms and war-cries shatter
hallucinating bony wars
And I remember nuns before the war

Forcento

It's gravity, spilling in capillaries, cheek-tissue trembling,
oozing past gravity to snuggle
Anne's rose-sweet gravity, and the stiff grave

I would go on coaxed by gravity and hard science.
But Gravity — and Expectation — and Fear —
and gravity, scientists say, is weak.

Moon-

Woman
the real sea snoring half a mile away
the scrubbed brick walls of the double lounge and its
samples of african drums flood the speakers

Is that your shadow, weightless,
a smudge of grey dust
in the black trickery of the she-oak?

the lyrebird
  in the moon,
with her cloudy skirt, shimmies down

Man
There are transparent fish
in the morning mist
        fish, coral
and offspring. The red is too brilliant,
big as Africa

or an infant at the telescope's opposite end

cattle walk over a hill, their eyes connected, swivelling
   now there is no safety anywhere

The moon will fizz like a pill in a drink …

Matrimonies

Their delicate armies sway
  the ambiguities of space.
Feel in your hands, before you play,

trembling in warmth, and rising,
the agitation of the strings.
It would be comforting to sing

    to the solid mercy of water.
Grasshoppers click and whirr.
    I am high on acid rock, on wandering glitter.

I feel your pulsebeat through my fingertips.
Look, where the grass grows more intense:
grows luminous in distance,

shaping my lips. I lie
    among dazzling visions, lying
to the fine edge of clarity:

The season for philosophy draws on.
Sparrows flock to my pond.
Verses flow in a never-ending torrent.

Death has no features of his own.
Music's much more than flesh and bone.
What's all this but the language of illusion?

Cyclone Songs

Prelude

Porch   wrecked,

     a back step's
        quasi sanctuary.

          Cups of tea,

warm butter, Vegespread
     on chargrilled bread.

          The day's
already ravaging like a scavenger.

     Bikes of green
ants glimmer.   Formication.

                    The atmos-
phere is magnified by sap.

          You're minuscule,
still spinning in that flinty,

squinting eye.   'Powerlessness!'
        skeins of generators announce.

Do you wish to record
  that fuming

Shu?   The only
surety's poetry.

Twenty-two's storming. Score
your cyclone   music.

You do what you can, or Eleven Steps

for Michelle Braunstein

rope the Queenslander's five tricolour windows
wind more, more between garage door and bumper
bump the porch's plants to the outside laundry
caution the grass of atomic coconuts
nut in the storeroom, pray to the starred goddess
oddly laugh: *There's a hurricane a-comin'*
accustom to flux the kitchen's stiff louvres
versify Pythagorean theorem
remove the pots and pans from appointed hooks
cook and freeze biodynamic tenderloins
coin 'The Sacrificial Chicken', huge ice cube

Doubleness, with anagrams

for Michele Sammut and Michael Scott

Feb 22, 37°C
Reddest day without power's veil   You're
deranged as the lost high
ways duplicating Bowie
's The Artist/Minotaur   In
this Year of the Sheep, Goat or Ram,
Tropical Cyclone Lam, Marcia's kid broth
er, dis sip ate s six hours before she dupes Rock
hampton, just north of the Tropic of Capricorn, ally
of two-faced Saturn   First time on record two CAT 4
storms strike Australia, same date   Tabloids magnif
y ***TWIN CYCLONES!***   Ruth & Martin loop Sett
lers of Catan: latent forecasts, you fold Clock
Solitaire: Ariel clicks too, Mulholland's
Tennis', matched volcanic peaks'
directions, get your
story straight about
this former central empire, 37-year-old
wildheart

Blessed be

the maggots
rimming the wheelie bin,
  their vehicle The Sacrificial Chicken

Hungry Jack's
piggy-
  backing the hospital's grid

the chainsaws
the rash of silver tongues, the silver toothes
  they know not what they do

the panic attack
that neither yoga nidra nor
  a rainy god can launder

Escuris Sardinas en Aceite de Oliva
served on soft bread: the candlelit dinner for two:
  precursor of Ticket to Ride: Europe

the poetry gods
to write or not to write
  to candlelight? the question is that

the generators
kleptomaniacs of sleep
  trumpety, a-buzz as 'The 13th'

Bees

At the highway's
torn hem,
              where mud crabs flense
pink dactyls,
                six dozen off-white boxes

Were you drawn by a love of
Porter, Duffy, Plath?
                    You are not a lover

of sweetness six-sided,
though such sweetness is as
dizzying as Virgil

You, the poet, took photographs,
the photographer sweated
spondees in the car
                    A worker,
positively charged,
tapped your shoulder
as this stillness taps your mind

Bursaria spinosa

> *You hold it like a lit bulb,*
> *a pound of light*
> —Jacob Polley

though technically it's less than a pound,
this Prickly Box, this jar of Unheated
Honey, gift from a haver hunting for
tinned tuna, thing to lighten your morning

cups of tea, to ball with tablespoons
under a swarming cluster, a waxing moon,
the only lit bulb in this city
where cops patrol broods of electricity

where you drone the common names: Australian
Boxthorn, Boxwood, Castanet Bush, Christmas
Bush, *Geapga*, *Kurwan*, Mock Orange, Native

Blackthorn, Native Box, Native Olive, Prick-
ly Pine, Spiny Box, Sweet Bursaria,
Thorn Box, Whitethorn, You're-Sick-To-Death-Of-Stars!

First Mail

av
    a
        lanche:
'De*live*ry!'

the contractor
rouses you from
    blackout

the Queenslander's
underfloor's explosive,
the Clark Rubber mattress
    adhesive

a chapbook's barcode's
tattooed a forearm

coconut water's
lukewarm sploosh

his uniform's Hypercolor-
    splotchy,
his B.O.'s a forerunner
of another bloody candlelit dinner

in this wasteland you envelop
the deck of Queen's Slipper,
    shear
cardboard like an emir

H is for Hawk comm-
emorates
Feb 24   chapter
one's etched

PATIENCE

Cyclone Songs

Hurricane

into the most inviolate room, a crocodile
of two   a transcendental
meditation
through louvres
slips Tutu

This Is Hardcore

your Hong Kong Orchid's
purple hearts are reversed in a neighbour's
front yard   shredded coconut
fronds, you embellish air

Pretend We're Dead

o

ll   o

a   n

the tables

b   s

have turned

from the bulwark-balustrade   / \

an out-of-time kookaburra's thunder-   e

bolt, butcherbirds' shrikelike habits   r

Marcia a kind of poultice   o

for the bulging   c

L4-L5   on the yoga mat your

The Power

17 middle-aged Tae Bo-ers
agitated a Seoul
Techno
Mart, July 5, 2011
39 storeys evacuated, as
after an earthquake
resonance recreated

The Horror Has Gone

~~my father's father's~~
~~atmospheres~~ ~~Ari~~
~~the Persian~~
~~bringer of rain~~
~~the brownouts of eternity~~

Blackout

after Kate Bush

Dark pizzicati
vision. The moon's tongue
silvers Babooshka.

The ice storm's

forming in Connect-i-cut, New Canaan.
At the Tropic of Capricorn, Land of Plenty,
louvres are weaving nine natural manes:

Camarillo horses with gilded reins.
An orange-parkaed boy's cavorting: a tempest's
forming in Connect-i-cut, New Canaan;

icicles chime moon boots: it's tempting fate
to walk the plank of a diving board at Silver Meadow.
Turn power and water off at the mains!

'… out of the past come the thundering hoofbeats of the great
horse Silver! The Lone Ranger rides …' from a neighbour's set.
Forming in Connect-i-cut, New Canaan:

'Mayday! Mayday! Get this message back to base!'
a malfunctioned toy soldier's endless
wave. The sea knows no end, especially Maine's.

Now, each downpipe houses a watergate.
The white horses are glimmering like Pegasus.
Formlessness in Connecticut, New Canaan.
Louvres have woven nine natural manes.

Coda

for Leigh Backhouse

Italian-born British opera singer Frederick Federici (April 22, 1850 – March 3, 1888) died at the conclusion of an opening-night performance of Faust *at the Princess Theatre, Melbourne.*

Between trapdoor and green-
room you died of your own horror,
a heart diseased, Mephistopheles.
So much for nitroglycerin,
galvanic battery. Subsequent opening
nights the Princess left vacant
one seat in the dress circle's third row,
the Theatre's utmost sign of respect.

*

Marshalling Mount Archer's
Xanthorrhoea, Great Keppel's
great whites, tigers and bulls,
you pursue under Artemis.
Chainsaws, lawnmower and weedeater
a lush quartet for this promised land
where a cyclone can harbour in
the palm of your hand.

In a Beautiful Place Out in the Country

Drums

Cyclone   's fade-out

Air-conditioned
library, south side

(even here the distinction
exists)   Multi-timbral

B.O., faulty aluminium
astringents   From 126

(9's √ your luckiest #) you accident
ally flam *that* poem

black ink a
(♪) prognosis

awareness a
hiss of snares:

Stop.   Plotting.

Cattle

A carcass with a milky
complexion idles at a red
light. A thousand pollarded
oracles couldn't carve a silky

purse for it. Its cow-brown eyes
low *The hide of death awaits*
these beasts … Unknowing's surprise.
Apollonian, we guard our fates.

Stern Man

for Nigel Featherstone

He knows he is rusting at the bottom
of the hollow barrel. When he strikes a
match, waits for kindling to catch, a peacock
drops larger pieces of wood inside. A

funnel's certain it must be 11
am. He immediately hears the
puff-puffing, becomes hotter, much hotter,
no longer dirty. The fire looks to be

out. Through the small windows, through the plane tree
branches, new lime-green leaves, it's no longer
winter. He stands naked for a moment,

eager for company, invites it, knows.
His heart is thumping hard inside his chest.
He leans his head onto the edge, eyes closed.

Mr Gingerlocks

The neoplasm, sleek, jet-black: *Why tend*
this sack of blood and bone pronounced too old
by Muscle Marys, periwigged? Pretend—
at 37, I'm out in the cold,

a subtle cub playing with the railings
of a broken rocker. The ascetics
may be on the money, flayers ailing
alone.
          Who fancies the antiseptic

touch of a whopping bore? I crave what lies
among Bornean trees (poachers unclean)—
a barbarian who snarls into skies,
not Fitness First's merciless eyes. O Mean

Girls, I crave not Tina, nor fey. Instead,
a Sun Bear to paw sweetness in my bed.

Cups

after Gwen Harwood

I know them by their lips. I know the proverb
about immediacy. Many slip
and shatter on sheer concrete, the older, the glass.
They held the common cold in hieratic,

are octopus-suckers. I imagine them
thus, lying facedown on acupuncture tables.
I apprehend firebirds. Their fearsome vacuum
surfaces disturbance. Flying saucers

might inscribe similar discs of stillness
in cereal: formations of purple, rose:
thirteen moons, an earth, a sun in syzygy.
They order qi, are venerable remedy.

They never play hard to get. Foul deed, foul day they aren't.
All bell, no whistle. Anti-insurrection.
A trance in sudsy buckets; rinsed, their lips
await others' blue skin. Love, their love is blind.

The Mixtape

First, only. TDK, *D90*.
I Feel Like A Dick ! Label golden
brown as heroin/es. Twenty years on
I taste *Tank Girl* and Jaffas, sticky
fingers purling mine, walking knitted,
dry-mouthed to that South Hobart flat, three
favourite songs ('Disco 2000',
'Roads', 'The 2 of Us'), score the clever
and the lonely double entendre.

In a Beautiful Place Out in the Country

for Benjamin Dodds

'Stew-art': singsong from the back
-yard: 'Ker-wik, they'll dissa-peer.'
You slip on his flip-flops, oversized,
slop to a drift of leaves: an egg sac,
pierced, a silken slap or milky smear,
start-stop hatchlings immortalised

by a mother cold before the rake
pried apart her hibiscus-fist's pledge,
ruffled the clutch of desiccated coconuts.
'The Aliens.' 'No, no, My Friend the Chocolate Cake
—Lime Spiders.' Masquerading as hedge,
golden canes can't restrain their mutts'

five o'clock shadows: three Baskerville
hounds whose harmonies whenever a siren
keens darkly over this better-on-paper cattle town
echo Bowen Basin's aggregate drill.
You back, dog-ear *Myron*,
down watered-down

Laphroaig. Paranoid
even kin will taste your heart
beat *uhth-er uhth-er*—the handsome women of Woody's
Supermarket, the Australia Post franchisee who intonates
    like the gilt droid
from *Star Wars* ('Locals' their designation, 'Swedeart'
yours, 'A*nuhth*er parcel of goodies')

—you flee the house,
a character actor (housemate's hand-feeding Jazz
Hands and Roxy now), bumble under Hong
Kong Orchid trees (*Not. My. Spouse.*
you mouth at the blue rinse weedeatering in a topaz
—your birthstone—muumuu), a song

voodooing headphones
(helical strings, apocalypse-vox), a doozy
: you glide over gravel like Marie Laveau,
or the way your physio's fingers glide over breastbones,
ladders to out-of-whack clavicles ('A brunette Chantoozie
once shouted me a bottle of red from Bordeaux'),

hook a left into the main drag,
pass the newsagency that doesn't sell
The Australian or *NME*
('Sooky fag.
Go back to Hell.'
: owner's mantra, *'Know thy self, know thy enemy'*

… 'Better the Devil You Know''s
nimbusing your best friend's parents' living room, he's
pogoing as you arrive:
regurgitated sherbert lacerates each nose;
it's a long way to Afghanistan from Wizz
Fizz …), ogle the Commodores that drive,

that drive; packed with underaged eyes blinking syn
-chronously—[YOUR] [FCKN] [DEDD] (Joe
Schmoe, you pulled the same shit inside a cousin's hotted-up Torana,
ripped on fear of a strike from the gear knob's red-back and Cyn
-di Lauper's *'fuh-uhn'*)—a white-hot model creeps obscenely slow,
like *Lantana*,

and at a crossroads comes to a stop
and its white-hot model creeps watch,
and their lids arise
and their mandibles drop
like zombies': Sasquatch
(frangipani-shimmer no disguise),

you swim to fluted bamboo
—underaged eyes' *dih*—but a
hybrid magpie's commandeering
the thunder-blue
and your mind's like pasteurised butter
and a coal train's squeal is endearing,

and scuttling home via Cellar
-brations you encounter, counting
spectra whilst reeling around a sprinkler,
awaiting
'Tea!' (or 'Dinner!'), a teenybopper,
the *ee-chong!* of a powder-coated swing.

Snowdrop in the Tropics

for Ruth Whebell and Martin Backhouse

A marvellous woman lives
in these treetops: poinciana, mango.
Three years ago a spinning wheel halved her sight,
doubled her vision.
She wears her eye-patch
charmingly. Parents, kids hook 'Pirate! Pirate!'

The woman's a snowdrop, irate
sometimes: parents, kids bear ideal lives,
she a black leather eye-patch
that silvers. Slivers of mango
glint in her kitchen. A vision
of a Uniting Church is a sight.

Sight … sight
is reality's pirate,
vision
the gardener of afterlives.
In the woman's garden each dignified mango
gleams like Marvel's Odin's eye-patch.

Her eye-patch
is heightening: it mostly dims unsight-
ly dropped vermilion flowers, rotting mango-
es: 'Pirate! Pirate!'
they bully from rookeries. 'Past lives
macaw!' proclaims a vision

of Victoria. In a welter of vision
the woman's a bonsai, patch-
ing the grumpy parents' lives, the lives
of the dopey kids: 'I'm happy, Doc, restoring sight
to the less than bashful pirate,
to the sneezy, sleepy mango-

nel.' Vermilion vexilla billowing hair, the mango
chutney maker bares Mason jars. 'A vision!'
twitters the President, who attempted to pirate
her recipe. 'Wish *I'd* a magical eye-patch,'
squawks the Secretary, envy desiccating sight.
The spinning wheel keels: the woman outlives

the CWA's mango chutney makers. With eye-patch
her vision's sharper than the spectacled flying fox's, her sight
more telescopic than the pirate's spyglass. Many are her lives.

Double Acrostic

after Ofelia Zepeda

The bird in my chest, a northern cardinal,
hosannaed the handsome paramedic who
electrocardiographed emu-
persona, New Year's Day. Windows carved

lenticular UFObjects on skies
abandoned as their desert creators. A
communion smiled me to The Base, a chair
extended bluely, I was rolled inside

where cannulae folded wings—Blastoff!
How white everything was! Wintry, though? No,
equatorial. No cut-paper
representation. Red sinkers absent from

extensive fields: white spaces: the place where
chaos yields to order, where clouds are formed.

Notes

The proem is a cento from nine of my poems: 'colour wheel', 'Black Cockatoos', 'Reflections', 'Fingal Valley', 'The Raising of the Dead', 'Bees', 'Horus and Set', 'Snowdrop in the Tropics', 'Cups'.

Reflections
'Ebon Cans': Gwen Harwood befriended me in the late 1980s, at All Saints Church, South Hobart; there, she would slip slim volumes of verse into my trouser pockets and insist I read and write poetry. Hers was a great voice, as of a trumpet.

'из России': *из России с любовью* is Russian for 'From Russia with love'; *Il y a un beau garçon là-bas* is French for 'There's a handsome boy over there'.

'ValproateFluoxetineClonazepam': Sodium valproate is used for the treatment of bipolar disorder; fluoxetine, major depressive and obsessive-compulsive disorder; clonazepam, panic disorder.

'another journey by train' samples Art Department's 'I C U' (words written and expressed by Kenneth F Glasgow), *The Drawing Board* (Crosstown Rebels, 2011). Used with kind permission of Kenneth F Glasgow. The title is borrowed from The Cure's song of the same name.

'Dissociation': Australia's Grim Reaper commercial was first screened on April 5, 1987.

‘ENDONE® Oxycodone hydrochloride 5 mg’ is a remix of the consumer medical information for ENDONE® oxycodone hydrochloride (http://www.mydr.com.au/medicines/cmis/endone-tablets).

‘Reflections’: The Cure played their first Reflections show (*Three Imaginary Boys*, *Seventeen Seconds*, *Faith*) at the Sydney Opera House on May 31, 2011.

‘The Rabbit Catcher’ is a remix of Sylvia Plath’s ‘The Rabbit Catcher’.

‘10.15 Saturday Night’: The title is borrowed from The Cure’s song of the same name.

‘The smile’s’: The phrase ‘that in my mind I’m sticking a fork into the back of my hand’ is a transformation of ‘I learned how to look cheerful while, under the table, I stuck a fork into the back of my hand’ from Stephen Frears’ *Dangerous Liaisons*.

‘i won’t let the sun go down on me’: The phrase ‘low on the highway roily & grey’ is a transformation of ‘The sky is low and gray, the roily gray of sliding surf’ from Don DeLillo’s *Underworld* (Picador, London, 1997).

Five Centos
I would like to express my deep gratitude to these poets who have inspired me and whose lines have comprised the following centos.

‘Cinquecento’ is a cento from Æmilia Lanyer’s ‘The Description of Cooke-ham’, Christopher Marlowe’s ‘Hero and Leander' and 'Elegies, Book One, 5', Isabella Whitney's 'A Communication Which the Author Had to London, Before She Made Her Will', John Donne's 'A Hymn to God the Father', Sir Philip Sidney's 'Ring Out Your Bells', Lady Mary Wroth's 'The Countesse of Montgomery's Urania: "Love peruse me, seeke, and finde"', George Gascoigne's 'The Steel Glass', John Skelton's 'To Mistress Margaret Hussey', Margaret Cavendish, Duchess of Newcastle-upon-Tyne's 'An Epilogue to the Above', William Shakespeare's 'Song of the Witches', Robert Southwell's 'New Heaven, New War', Mary Sidney Herbert's '*O*', Sir Thomas Wyatt's 'Avising the Bright Beams' and Richard Barnfield's 'Sonnet 17'.

'Walking Wounded' is a cento. 'A land where war seems impossible' is from Mark O'Connor's 'Bogongs', *The Olive Tree: Collected Poems 1972–2000* (Hale & Iremonger, Alexandria, NSW, 2000). Used with kind permission of Hale & Iremonger. 'I have carried within me a war, and scars,' is from Julian Croft's 'After a war (any war)', *Ocean Island* (John Leonard Press, Elwood, Vic., 2006). Used with kind permission of Julian Croft. 'a blue sepulchral war and secret' is from Gig Ryan's 'Alba', *Pure and Applied* (Craftsman House and Paper Bark Press, Brooklyn, NSW, 1998). Used with kind permission of Gig Ryan. 'men-o'-war' is from Stephen K Kelen's 'Mosquito Dreaming', *Dingo Sky* (ETT Imprint, Sydney, 1993). Used with kind permission of ETT Imprint. 'a greed for war like love' is from Vincent Buckley's 'Soft War Poems', *Last Poems* (McPhee Gribble, Carlton, Vic., 1991). Used with kind permission of Penguin Random House Australia. 'a frail society scattered by war repeatedly overrun' is from Lee Cataldi's 'the fortunes of war', *The Women Who Live on the Ground: Poems 1978–1988* (Penguin, Ringwood, Vic.,

1990). Used with kind permission of Lee Cataldi. 'We play war games on the verandahs' is from Dorothy Hewett's 'War Hero', *Halfway up the Mountain* (Fremantle Press, North Fremantle, WA, 2001). Used with kind permission of Fremantle Press. 'of rare champagne, war songs,' is from David Malouf's 'A Classroom in the Fifties', *Poems 1959–1989* (UQP, St Lucia, Qld, 1992). Used with kind permission of David Malouf. 'war wounds — or something like that …' is from Diane Fahey's 'The Third Day' from the sequence 'Bluebeard's Wife' in *The Sixth Swan* (Five Islands Press, Wollongong, NSW, 2001), where it follows these lines: 'At dawn's first watery flare / he'd clumped in, thrown the circle / of keys onto her lap. Yes, / he'd been absent for a while — / business, a trip to the coast, // specialist doctors for his /'. Used with kind permission of Diane Fahey. 'You say you mean peace: I say' is from Stefanie Bennett's 'Voices from "The Islands of the Blest"', *Radio City 2 a.m.* (Cochon Publishing, North Ward, Qld, 1976). Used with kind permission of Stefanie Bennett. 'peace, blackmail' is from Lionel Fogarty's 'I Sus I', *Minyung Woolah Binnung: What Saying Says* (Keeaira Press, Southport, Qld, 2004). 'And bangs and booms and war-cries shatter' is from Nancy Cato's 'War and Peace', *The Dancing Bough* (Angus and Robertson, Sydney, 1957). 'hallucinating bony wars' is from Luke Davies' 'Jason and the Argonauts', *Absolute Event Horizon* (Angus and Robertson, Sydney, 1994). Used with kind permission of HarperCollins Australia. 'And I remember nuns before the war' is from Vivian Smith's 'The Restorers', *New Selected Poems* (Angus and Robertson, Sydney, 1995). Used with kind permission of HarperCollins Australia.

'Forcento' is a cento. 'It's gravity, spilling in capillaries, cheek-tissue trembling,' is from Anne Winters' 'The Mill-Race', *The*

Displaced of Capital (University of Chicago Press, Chicago, 2004). Used with kind permission of University of Chicago Press. 'oozing past gravity to snuggle' is an excerpt from 'Venus and the Ark' from *To Bedlam and Part Way Back* by Anne Sexton. Copyright © 1960 by Anne Sexton, renewed 1988 by Linda G Sexton. Reprinted by permission of the Estate of Anne Sexton c/o Sterling Lord Literistic, and Houghton Mifflin Harcourt Publishing Company. All rights reserved. 'Anne's rose-sweet gravity, and the stiff grave' is from Margaret Avison's 'New Year's Poem', *Always Now: The Collected Poems* (The Porcupine's Quill, Erin, Ontario, 2003). Used with kind permission of The Porcupine's Quill. 'I would go on coaxed by gravity and hard science.' is from 'Invention' from *Half-Lit Houses* © 2004 by Tina Chang. Reprinted with permission of Four Way Books. All rights reserved. 'But Gravity — and Expectation — and Fear —' is from Emily Dickinson's 'Unit, like Death, for Whom?', first published in *New England Quarterly*, 1947. 'and gravity, scientists say, is weak.' is from Jane Hirshfield's 'For What Binds Us', *Of Gravity & Angels*, published by Wesleyan University Press, copyright © 1988 Jane Hirshfield. Used by permission of Wesleyan University Press.

'Moon-' is a cento. 'the real sea snoring half a mile away' is from Alison Clark's 'To the Moon Behind Branches', *About Desire and other poems* (William Heinemann, Port Melbourne, Vic., 1996). Used with kind permission of Alison Clark. 'the scrubbed brick walls of the double lounge and its' is from joanne burns' 'moon', *penelope's knees* (UQP, St Lucia, Qld, 1996). Used with kind permission of joanne burns. 'samples of african drums flood the speakers' is from Jill Jones' 'waiting for the moon beyond the disco', *Flagging Down Time* (Five Islands Press, Wollongong, NSW, 1993).

Used with kind permission of Jill Jones. 'Is that your shadow, weightless,' is from Dorothy Hewett's 'Moon-Man', *Selected Poems* (Fremantle Press, South Fremantle, WA, 1991). Used with kind permission of Fremantle Press. 'a smudge of grey dust' is from Nicolette Stasko's 'The Moth and the Moon', *Glass Cathedrals: New and Selected Poems* (Salt Publishing, Cambridge, UK, 2006). Used with kind permission of Nicolette Stasko. 'in the black trickery of the she-oak?' is from Caroline Caddy's 'Editing the Moon', *Editing the Moon* (Fremantle Press, South Fremantle, WA, 1999). Used with kind permission of Fremantle Press. 'the lyrebird' is from Kate Llewellyn's 'Speaking of the Moon'. Used with kind permission of Tim Curnow Literary Agent, Sydney. 'in the moon,' is from Dorothy Porter's 'Full Moon', *Akhenaten* (UQP, St Lucia, Qld, 1992). Used with kind permission of Andrea Goldsmith. 'with her cloudy skirt, shimmies down' is from MTC Cronin's 'Sonnet of Eggs & Moons', *Everything Holy* (Balcones International Press, Temple, Texas, 1998). Used with kind permission of MTC Cronin. 'There are transparent fish' is from Gary Catalano's 'Nocturnes', *Selected Poems 1973–1992* (UQP, St Lucia, Qld, 1993). Used with kind permission of Helen Hewitt. 'in the morning mist' is from Julian Croft's '1978', *Loose Federation* (Kardoorair Press, Armidale, NSW, 1979). Used with kind permission of Julian Croft. 'fish, coral' is from Stephen K Kelen's 'Moon Beach', *Shimmerings: Poems* (Five Islands Press, Wollongong, NSW, 2000). Used with kind permission of Stephen K Kelen. 'and offspring. The red is too brilliant,' is from John Kinsella's 'The Healing Of The Circle', *Full Fathom Five* (Fremantle Press, South Fremantle, WA, 1993). Used with kind permission of Clive Newman, Writers' Agent. 'big as Africa' is from Mark O'Connor's 'Moon over Mindil Beach', *The Forever Lands:*

Australia's Northern Territory in words and images (Beyond Images, Camberwell East, Vic., 2000). Used with kind permission of Mark O'Connor. 'or an infant at the telescope's opposite end' is from Alex Skovron's 'A Concise History of the Moon', *The Rearrangement* (Melbourne University Press, Carlton, Vic., 1988). Used with kind permission of Alex Skovron. 'cattle walk over a hill, their eyes connected, swivelling' is from Michael Dransfield's 'Philosophy of movement', *Collected Poems* (UQP, St Lucia, Qld, 1987). Used with kind permission of UQP. 'now there is no safety anywhere' is from 'Diana and Actaeon' from *Collected Poems* by Peter Porter. Published by Oxford University Press, 1989. Copyright © Peter Porter. Reproduced by the permission of the Estate of Peter Porter c/o Rogers, Coleridge & White Ltd., 20 Powis Mews, London W11 1JN. 'The moon will fizz like a pill in a drink …' is from Alan Gould's 'Moon', *The Past Completes Me: Selected Poems 1973–2003* (UQP, St Lucia, Qld, 2005). Used with kind permission of UQP.

'Matrimonies' is a cento from Gwen Harwood. 'Their delicate armies sway' is from 'Reed Voices', *Selected Poems* (Penguin Random House Australia, North Ryde, NSW, 1990). 'the ambiguities of space.' is from 'The Wasps', *Selected Poems.* 'Feel in your hands, before you play,' is from 'A Music Lesson', *Selected Poems.* 'trembling in warmth, and rising,' is from 'Songs of Eve I', *Collected Poems 1943–1995* (UQP, St Lucia, Qld, 2013). 'the agitation of the strings.' is from 'Moonlight', *Collected Poems 1943–1995.* 'It would be comforting to sing' is from 'An Old Graveyard', *Collected Poems 1943–1995.* 'to the solid mercy of water.' is from 'Looking towards Bruny', *Collected Poems 1943–1995.* 'Grasshoppers click and whirr.' is from 'Carnal Knowledge II', *Selected Poems.* 'I am high on acid rock, on wandering glitter.' is from 'Mappings of the Plane', *Selected Poems*. 'I feel your pulsebeat through my fingertips.' is from 'Night Thoughts: Baby & Demon', *Selected Poems*. 'Look, where the grass grows more intense:' is from 'Oyster Cove Pastorals', *Selected Poems*. 'grows luminous in distance,' is from 'Shellgrit', *Collected Poems 1943–1995*. 'shaping my lips. I lie' is from 'Dust to Dust', *Selected Poems*. 'among dazzling visions, lying' is from 'Night Flight', *Selected Poems*. 'to the fine edge of clarity:' is from 'Littoral', *Selected Poems*. 'The season for philosophy draws on.' is from 'Thoughts before Sunrise', *Collected Poems 1943–1995*. 'Sparrows flock to my pond.' is from 'Three Poems for Margaret Diesendorf', *Selected Poems*. 'Verses flow in a never-ending torrent.' is from 'A Public Place', *Collected Poems 1943–1995*. 'Death has no features of his own.' is from 'Death Has No Features of His Own', *Selected Poems*. 'Music's much more than flesh and bone.' is from 'A Music Lesson', *Selected Poems*. 'What's all this but the language of illusion?' is from 'After a Dream', *Collected Poems 1943–1995*. Lines from *Selected Poems* used with kind permission of Penguin Random House Australia; lines from *Collected Poems 1943–1995* used with kind permission of John Harwood.

Cyclone Songs

Tropical Cyclone Marcia traversed over Rockhampton, Queensland as a Category 3 system on February 20, 2015.

'Prelude' was written after reading Cameron Lowe's *Porch Music*.

'You do what you can, or Eleven Steps' samples *The Golden Girls*.

‘*Bursaria spinosa*’: The epigraph ‘You hold it like a lit bulb, a pound of light’ is from Jacob Polley’s ‘A Jar of Honey’, *The Brink* (Picador, London, 2003). Used with kind permission of Pan Macmillan UK.

‘Cyclone Songs’: The section titles are borrowed from Grace Jones’ ‘Hurricane’, Pulp’s ‘This Is Hardcore’, L7’s ‘Pretend We’re Dead’, Snap!’s ‘The Power’ and Antony and the Johnsons’ ‘The Horror Has Gone’.

‘The ice storm’s’ samples *The Lone Ranger*, and was written after watching Ang Lee’s *The Ice Storm* and reading ‘Since Unfinished’, a poem by Richard Blanco.

In a Beautiful Place Out in the Country

‘Stern Man’ is a remix of the proem from Nigel Featherstone’s *Remnants*.

‘Cups’ is a transformation of Gwen Harwood’s ‘Cups’.

‘The Mixtape’: ‘Golden Brown’ is a song by The Stranglers.

‘In a Beautiful Place Out in the Country’: The title is borrowed from the Boards of Canada EP of the same name. In *Birds of Australia*, Ken Simpson and Nicholas Day describe the voice of the Rufous Whistler as a ‘[r]inging, whipcrack “ee-chong!”’.

‘Double Acrostic’: The phrase ‘cut-paper’ is from Sylvia Plath’s ‘Tulips’.

Acknowledgements

I would like to thank the editors of *Assaracus: A Journal of Gay Poetry* (USA), *Australian Book Review*, *Australian Poetry Anthology 2015* (eds Sarah Holland-Batt and Brook Emery), *Blackmail Press* (NZ), *Blue Dog*, *The Canberra Times*, *Communion*, *Cordite Poetry Review*, *foam:e*, *fourW twenty-three*, *fourW twenty-four*, *Going Down Swinging*, *HIV Here & Now Project*, *Island Magazine*, *Mascara Literary Review*, *Meanjin*, *Overland*, *Plumwood Mountain*, *Poem and Dish*, *Rabbit Poetry Journal*, *Regime 04*, *Seizure*, *Snorkel*, *The Fractured Self: Poetry of Chronic Illness and Pain* (ed. Heather Taylor Johnson), *The Lifted Brow*, *The Warwick Review* (UK), *The Weekend Australian*, *Transnational Literature*, *Westerly* and *Writ Poetry Review*, in which many of these poems first appeared, some in earlier versions, or are forthcoming.

*

… one may chop wood, make bricks, forge iron without love, but one can no more deal with people without love than one can handle bees without care.
—Leo Tolstoy, *Resurrection*

Immeasurable thanks to my editor Felicity Plunkett for her kindness, vision and intuition (and for trusting mine); to my publisher Madonna Duffy for her open-mindedness; and to Ian See and the UQP team for their eagerness, warmth and expertise.

Grazie mille Benjamin 'BMD' Dodds for guidance and laughter, and for reading and commenting on these and many other poems; Matt Hetherington and Ric Hool for advice and close reading of an earlier version of the manuscript; Chris and Bob Mole, swiftest, wittiest carrier pigeons; Ali Alizadeh, Amanda Anastasi, William Ayot, Ashley Capes, Verity Charlton, Mary Chydiriotis, Justin Clemens, Phillip A Ellis, Mira Gojak, Stu Hatton, Mark William Jackson, Alexis Lateef, Justin Lowe, Annerliegh Grace McCall, Julie Maclean, Nathanael O'Reilly, Peter Rose, Silvia Schivella, Thomas Shapcott, Sjón and Jessica L Wilkinson, among others, for timely encouragement.

Special thanks to Carol Ann Duffy for reading and commenting on 'Dissociation' and 'Glasshouses'.

Thank you to my teachers for their determination and firm belief, especially Berenice Eastman, Gwen Harwood, Amanda Jackson, Jeffrey Kelly, Liz McQuilkin, Adam O'Mara, Deborah Rechter and Bree Weizenegger.

Deepest gratitude and plainsong to my family and friends for their inspiration, anchorage and aid, especially Marie Barnes, Gary Barnes, Deb Reynolds and Mel Penglase, Simon Ancher, Leigh, Martin, Noel and Vallis Backhouse, Donna Bowman, Michelle Braunstein, Anthony Hack and Willa Hack, Simone Demanuele, Adrian English, Nigel Featherstone, Malcolm Grant, Anthony 'Goo' Hasell and Jason Parkinson, Alison Hasell, Zachary Humphrey, Anthony Jarvis, Kriyavidya and George Worthy, Peter Little, Relle McFarlane, Richard McLean, Andrew and Rob McQuilkin, Sandy Mitchell, David Musolino, Josh Nester, Andrew Norris, BN (Bruce) Oakman, Rishad Patel, Robert Pearce, Natalia Ramirez, Michele Sammut, Michael

Scott, Dan Stainsby, Therese 'T' Stuart, Michelle Sweeney, Anna Timou, Katie Watmough, Ruth and Melissa Whebell, and Daniel Young.

Cellosong for Phyllis Braslin, Nancy, Mervyn and Greg Barnes, Matthew John Davies, Rhonda Jancovic, Kerry Jeffers and Shane Maxwell.

Other volumes by Thomas Shapcott Poetry Prize winners

EATING MY GRANDMOTHER: A GRIEF CYCLE
Krissy Kneen

I pick a grain of her, stolen from the urn
place it on my tongue.
Her body.
My blood.

She lodges in me.

Bereft after her grandmother's death, Krissy Kneen began writing these poems in an attempt to make sense of her loss. This powerful work offers a kaleidoscope of fitful dreams, tender memories and heart-struck musings that shine new light on our own mortality.

> '*Eating My Grandmother* is a powerful memento mori that honours [Kneen's] grandmother and reminds us of our own proximity to dust.' *The Big Issue*

> 'Raw and exhilarating, *Eating My Grandmother* embodies the visceral paradox of grief.' Kristina Olsson

> 'At once exquisitely sensitive and blazing with wit and experimentation, Kneen re-imagines elegiac poetry.'
> Judges' comments, Thomas Shapcott Poetry Prize

ISBN 978 0 7022 5374 4

UQP

www.ingramcontent.com/pod-product-compliance
Ingram Content Group UK Ltd.
Pitfield, Milton Keynes, MK11 3LW, UK
UKHW021443041225
9375UKWH00032B/757

9 780702 254130